It Pay Back Time

by Jan Weeks

illustrated by Steven Bray

STANLEY THORNES

The Characters

Daniel
That's me.

Luke and Chris
The terrible Perkins twins.

Nerida
They have a sister.

The Setting

CONTENTS

Chapter 1
Two Against One 2

Chapter 2
Ruckus Goes Missing . . 10

Chapter 3
Beachcombing 18

Chapter 4
Are You Really
a Genie? 22

Chapter 5
The Wish 30

Chapter 6
Time to Go Home 44

CHAPTER 1

Two Against One

I used to like going to stay at the seaside, until the Perkins twins moved in next door.

Mr and Mrs Perkins are OK. Mr Perkins rides a motor bike. Sometimes he gives me a ride.

It's their terrible twins, Luke and Chris, that I can't stand.

"Give me a go on your boogie board, Daniel," Luke says when he sees me on the beach. "If you don't, I'll flatten your nose and punch your lights out."

Chris doesn't even bother to ask. He grabs my board and runs into the water, laughing. If I try to get it back, he pushes me under the waves and sits on me.

Their boogie boards look like they came from the rubbish tip. By the time they get through with mine, it will look the same. There are already scratches on it and big bits missing from the sides.

Nerida is the twins' little sister.
She would like to hang around me all the time.

"Can I play with Daniel?" she asks my mum a million times a day.

Good old Mum. She tries to help. "I think Daniel is busy right now," she always answers.

Then Nerida says, "Can I come in and wait?"

Being loved by Nerida is almost as bad as being bashed by her brothers.

CHAPTER 2

Ruckus Goes Missing

The Perkins have a dog called Ruckus. Yesterday someone let Ruckus off his lead. No-one knew where he'd gone.

Mr Perkins needs Ruckus to guard his motor bike. He said the twins should have tied him up properly so they had to look for him.

The twins spent hours climbing the hills and calling the dog's name. But they didn't find him.

When they came back, the twins blamed me. They thought I let Ruckus off his lead. It's because I told Nerida I didn't like their dog. He's always barking at me.

"I didn't touch your silly dog," I said to them. "He must have chewed through the rope."

"Your trainer was near his kennel. That means it had to be you," Chris answered.

As if that was proof! Ruckus was always stealing things.

Dad asked me to go to the shop to get some bread. Chris and Luke were coming back from the beach. They had found Ruckus. The three of them chased me all the way home.

"You come back here!" they shouted.

I had to think of a way to pay them back.

CHAPTER 3

Beachcombing

Today the sun was shining so I headed down to the beach. There was lots of seaweed and junk washed up on the sand.

I was dragging a stick behind me when it hit something hard. I looked down and saw a shiny object in the sand.

It was a green, metal bottle. It was round at the bottom with a long, skinny neck. I unscrewed the lid.

Smoke floated out and formed a shape next to me. The shape turned into a little man.

My mouth fell open. I couldn't believe my eyes. I'd found a bottle with a genie in it.

CHAPTER 4

Are You Really a Genie?

The little man didn't look like a genie. "What are you staring at?" he asked, folding his arms and glaring at me.

"Are you really a genie?" I asked.

"You saw me come out of the bottle, didn't you?" he replied. "Why are you bothering me? I've been in that bottle for a thousand years and I have things to do."

I'd set the genie free. Wasn't he supposed to grant me three wishes?

"I am your master now," I said. "You must do what I tell you."

"Who told you that?" he said and laughed at me.

"Everyone knows a genie must obey his master," I said.

"Nobody told me," answered the genie, "so, good-bye!" And with that, he floated back into the bottle.

I turned the bottle upside down and shook it.

"Go away!" he shouted. "You're making me dizzy."

"You had better come out," I told him. "If you don't, I'll fill your bottle with water and drown you."

"Put me down," he answered, "or I'll turn you into a three-headed toad and feed you to the sharks."

"You can't do that to me," I said. "I am your master."

"Oh, very well," he sighed. "You can have one wish."

CHAPTER 5

The Wish

"Come on! Make it snappy," grumbled the genie. "I don't have all day."

I made up my mind. I wanted him to make me invisible.

Shazam!

I looked down. Where my body used to be there was nothing! No legs, no body, no arms. Was this how a ghost felt?

I raced home singing, "Hi ho! Hi ho! No-one can see where I go. And when you can't be seen, no-one can see where you've been."

Dad was in the backyard hanging out the towels. I decided to have some fun. Every time Dad bent over to grab some pegs, I threw the towel he'd put on the line, back into the basket.

When he went to tell Mum, I pegged out all the towels.

"Maybe you should stay out of the sun," Mum said to Dad. "I think you are seeing things."

When she went back inside, I sprayed Dad with the hose. He went inside mumbling to himself.

I could hear Ruckus barking. He was tied up under a tree. I gently pulled his tail. He ran around in circles.

I bounced his ball in front of him.
I crawled inside his kennel and banged
on it from the inside.

Ruckus lay down and put his paws over his eyes.

Inside the Perkins' house, they were all having lunch. The kids all had glasses of cola. Luke drank his in one gulp.

I poured Chris' cola into Luke's glass. When Chris saw that his glass was empty, he grabbed Luke's full one. It slipped and cola went all over Nerida's spaghetti.

Nerida screamed, "Mum, look what Chris did!"

Mrs Perkins went to get Nerida another lunch.

I then tipped Luke's spaghetti over his head. It looked like orange worms.

Luke thought that Chris had done it. He got up and started a fight with Chris. Pow! Pow!

"Go to your bedroom," Mr Perkins roared, "and stay there until I tell you to come out."

It was the most fun I'd had in ages.

CHAPTER 6

Time to Go Home

At my house we were having pizza. It smelt so good. Mum had cut a slice for me but I couldn't eat it ... not while they were sitting there.

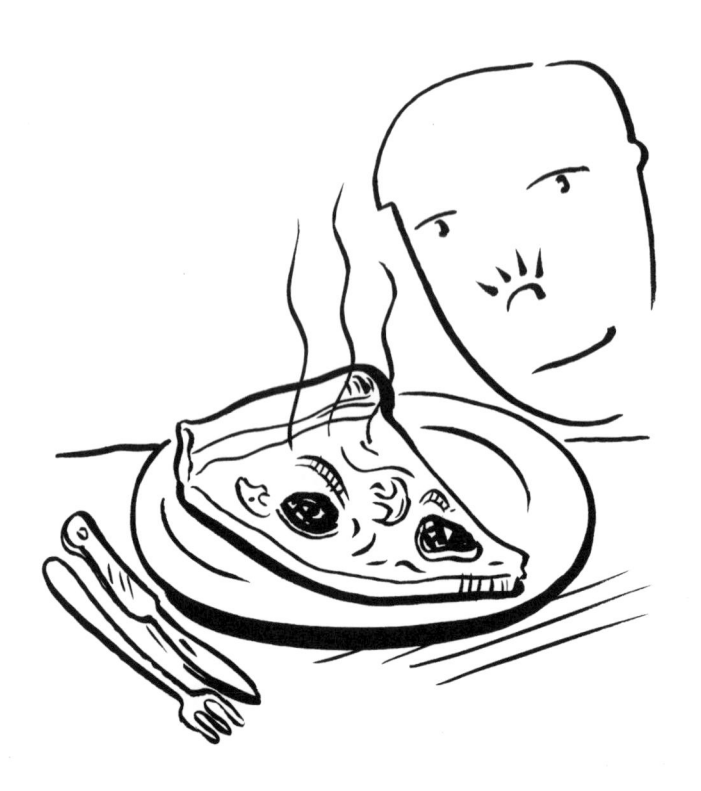

I was so hungry. I waited until they weren't looking and took a big bite.
It tasted so good I took another bite.

"Why are you eating Daniel's pizza?" Mum asked Dad.

"I'm not," Dad answered, shaking his head. "I don't believe the things that are happening today."

"I wonder where Daniel can be?" Mum asked. "It's not like him to miss pizza. I hope nothing has happened to him."

Later that day they really began to worry about me. They went next door to the Perkins' house. The twins didn't want to search for me.

"Who cares if he's lost?" they grumbled.

I followed them all to the beach.
Mum was so sad and Dad was upset.
It made me wish I'd never become
invisible.

They hadn't gone far when Chris found the genie's bottle.

"Catch, Luke," he said, throwing it to his brother.

"Bet I can throw it higher than you," Luke said, tossing the bottle into the air.

"Bet you can't!"

I had to do something. I had to get that bottle back before they opened it.

I was afraid that I might never become visible again. Snatching it from Chris, I raced along the beach. I unscrewed the lid.

"I don't want to be invisible any more," I shouted down the neck of the bottle.

"Too bad," the genie answered. "That was your wish. Go away."

"You have to help me," I sobbed. "Please, Genie."

The genie poked his head out of the bottle.

"Very well," he said. "You can have a second wish, but only if you promise to throw my bottle back into the sea."

I promised.

He did his trick and I was visible again. I could see me again ... my legs, my arms, everything.

The little man went back into his bottle. I put the lid on, climbed up onto some rocks and threw the bottle far out to sea.

Mum and Dad came running over to me. After hugging and kissing me all over I got into big trouble for making them worry. I didn't care. I was just happy to be back.

GLOSSARY

beachcombing
hunting for good things (treasure) on a beach

boogie board
a small foam surf board

bothering
very annoying; being a pest

floated
drifted along in the air

genie
a magic person who lives in a bottle

grumbled
complained in a low cranky voice

guard
to look after

invisible
something which is there but you cannot see it

obey
to do what you are told

visible
something which can be easily seen

Jan Weeks

What is your favourite breakfast?
> **French toast and heaps of crunchy bacon.**

Who is your favourite cartoon character?
> **The Road Runner.**

What was your least favourite activity at school?
> **Algebra.**

Why is the sky blue?
> **When God finished painting the sea He had lots of blue paint left over and, being an economical kind of superior being, decided to use it to paint the sky.**

Steven Bray

What is your favourite breakfast?
> **Fish fingers.**

Who is your favourite cartoon character?
> **Homer Simpson.**

What was your least favourite activity at school?
> **Maths.**

Why is the sky blue?
> **Because white clouds look their best against blue.**